About the Author

Mr. Sagar Salunke has 10 years of experience in automation testing including QTP(UFT) and Selenium Webdriver in VB.Net. He has worked on large investment banking projects in tier-1 Software Companies in India, USA, UK, Australia and Switzerland.

He has designed automation frameworks in Selenium with VB.Net that is widely used in the IT industry.

His hobbies include travelling to new tourist places, watching basketball, cricket and learning latest technological stuff.

A special note of Thanks to My Wife

I would like to dedicate this book to my lovely wife Priyanka for loving me so much and helping me write this book. Without her support, this book would not have been a reality.

Preface

These days lot of web applications are being developed to meet the growing demands of business.

So testing these applications is a big challenge. Automating test scenarios has become almost inevitable to reduce the overall cost and fast regression testing.

Selenium webdriver is the best open source testing framework that can be used to automate the testing activities in web application project.

In this book I have included all webdriver concepts with examples in VB.Net.

For latest updates on selenium webdriver, you can visit my blog at below url.

http://www.selenium-interview-questions.blogspot.com

You can write to me at reply2sagar@gmail.com and you can join my facebook network at
https://www.facebook.com/sagar.salunke.186

Table of Contents

About the Author 0

1. SELENIUM Basics 6

    1.1. What is Selenium? 6

    1.2. What is selenium webdriver? 6

    1.3. Browsers supported by Selenium. 6

    1.4. Choosing technology for selenium. 7

    1.5. Installing selenium with VB.Net. 7

2. First Script in Selenium Webdriver 10

    2.1. Sample Program 13

    2.2. Explaination 15

3. Identifying the elements in SELENIUM 17

    3.1.Xpath 17

    3.2.CSS 21

    3.3.LinkText 23

    3.4.Name 23

    3.5.Id 23

    3.6.Class Name 24

    3.7.Tag Name 24

    3.8.Partial Link Text 25

4. Performing User Actions in Selenium 26

    4.1. Entering data in Editboxes 26

    4.2. Selecting a value from the Combo boxes 27

4.3. Clicking on Web Buttons in 29

4.4.Clicking on links 31

4.5.Setting on/off checkboxes 33

4.6. Selecting the radiobutton 35

5. Reading data from webpage in Selenium..................... 37

5.1.Reading data from Editboxes 38

5.2.Reading data from combo boxes 40

5.3.Reading data from checkboxes 42

5.4.Reading data from Radio Buttons........................ 44

5.5.Working with Tables in SELENIUM........................... 47

6. Synchronization in SELENIUM....................................... 48

6.1. Page Load Synchrnoization 48

6.2. Element Synchronization 48

6.3. Synchronization based upon specific condition..... 48

7. Advanced Operations in Selenium............................... 50

7.1. Mouse Events in SELENIUM 50

7.2.Taking Screen shots in SELENIUM 51

7.3.Executing Java Script in SELENIUM 53

8. Frames, Alerts and Windows in SELENIUM 55

8.1. Handling Frames.. 55

8.2.Working with Alerts and Windows 56

9. Important Built-in Function in VB.Net. 59

9.1. Working with Strings in VB.Net.............................. 59

9.2. Working with Date and Time 62

9.3. Working with Files and Folders 63

9.4. Maths.. 64

10. Exception Handling in SELENIUM............................. 66

11. Excel Programming in SELENIUM 68

11.1. Creating and writing data to Excel Workbook 68

11.2. Reading data from existing workbook 70

12. Framework Designing in SELENIUM 72

1. SELENIUM Basics

1.1. What is Selenium?

Selenium is the open source web application testing framework released under apache license. Selenium can be installed on

1. Windows
2. Linux
3. Macintosh.

It supports programming in many languages as mentioned below.

1. VB.Net (C#.Net, J#)
2. Java
3. PHP
4. Ruby
5. Python
6. Perl

1.2. What is selenium webdriver?

Selenium WebDriver is the successor to Selenium RC. In earlier versions of selenium we needed Selenium RC server to execute the test scripts.
Now we can use webdriver to execute the test on particular browser. For each browser we have a separate web driver which accepts the selenium commands and drives the browser under test.

1.3. Browsers supported by Selenium.

Below is the list of browsers supported by the selenium webdriver.

1. Internet Explorer
2. Google Chrome
3. Firefox
4. Opera
5. Safari

Please note that for each browser, there is a separate web driver implementation.

1.4. Choosing technology for selenium.

As mentioned earlier, there are lot of languages that can be used for selenium scripting. Choosing the language depends upon the below factors.

1. Skill Set of employees in the organisation.
2. Training required on specific language.

I have selected VB.Net as a programming language for selenium scripting. So in this book you will see all examples in VB.Net only. But the same applies to other languages with some syntactical differences.

1.5. Installing selenium with VB.Net.

Well – Now let us understand the installation steps in selenium.

The list of Softwares you will need is given below.

1. Microsoft Visual Studio Express Edition
   http://www.visualstudio.com/en-us/downloads/download-visual-studio-vs
2. Selenium VB.Net API (dll file)
   @http://docs.seleniumhq.org/download/

3. Web driver for Chrome (exe file)

@https://code.google.com/p/selenium/downloads/list

Language	Client Version	Release Date			
Java	2.40.0	2014-02-19	Download	Change log	Javadoc
C#	2.40.0	2014-02-19	Download	Change log	API docs
Ruby	2.40.0	2014-02-19	Download	Change log	API docs
Python	2.40.0	2014-02-19	Download	Change log	API docs
Javascript (Node)	2.40.0	2014-02-19	Download	Change log	API docs

Figure 1 - C# and VB.Net Bindings for Selenium

Please note that Selenium API for C# and VB.net is same.

Once you have these softwares with you, You can follow below steps.

- Open VB 2010 express.
- Create a new project with name SampleTest in it.
- Go to project properties, right click and select add references. Browse to the dll file you have downloaded in the 2 step.
- click ok.

You can take help of the visual studio expert on how to do this.

Below image shows how to configure the visual studio for selenium webdriver project. You have to add the reference of the webdriver.dll to current vb.net project.

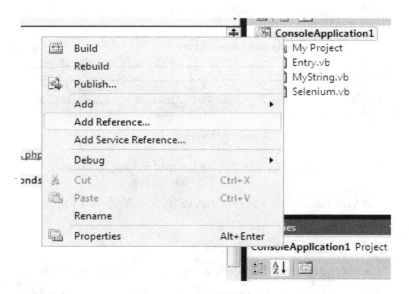

Figure 2 - Adding the selenium dll reference

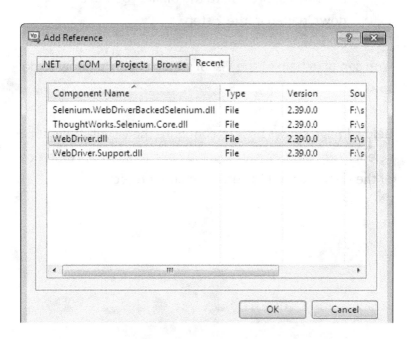

Figure 3 - Add WebDriver.dll to project

2. First Script in Selenium Webdriver

Before I jump to first script in selenium webdriver, let me tell you how you can use developer tools provided by browsers like IE, chrome, firefox while automating the web applications.

Inspecting Elements in Google Chrome.

Google chrome provides very nice tool to inspect the elements on the webpage. You have to just right click on the web element and then select last menu item from the context menu – Inspect. After you click on it, You will see the source code of that element as displayed in below image.

When you take your mouse over the code, correspodning elements on the webpage are highlighted. So it is very easy to identify the elements on the webpage.

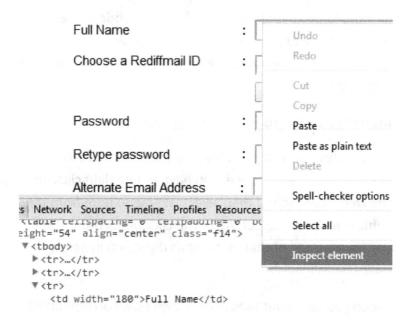

Figure 4 - Inspecting Elements in Chrome

Inspecting Elements in Internet Explorer.

Internet Explorer 10 and higher provides the developer tools from wehre you can inspect the elements on the webpage. You have to click on the arrow (circled in th red) and then click on the element on the webpage as displayed in below image.

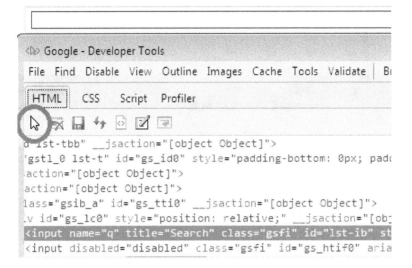

Figure 5 - Inspecting Elements in IE

Inspecting Elements in FireFox.

Inspecting elements in firefox is similar to chrome. Inspecting elements will help you knowing the attributes of the elements like name, id etc. which in turn can be used in selenium scripts.

Figure 6 - Inspecting element in Firefox

Let us start with scripting right away. Have a look at below example.

2.1. Sample Program

```vb
Imports System
Imports System.Collections.Generic
Imports System.Linq
Imports System.Text
Imports System.Threading
Imports OpenQA.Selenium
Imports OpenQA.Selenium.Firefox
Imports OpenQA.Selenium.Chrome
Imports OpenQA.Selenium.IE
'Imports OpenQA.Selenium.Support.UI
Imports System.Collections.ObjectModel

Module Module1
```

13

```vbnet
Sub Main()
    Dim driver As IwebDriver
        driver = Nothing

    Try

        driver = New
ChromeDriver("F:\selenium\csharp")

        driver.Url = http://www.google.co.in

        driver.Manage().Window.Maximize()

        driver.Navigate()

    Catch e As Exception

        Console.WriteLine("Exception .**{0}",
e.ToString())

    Finally

            Thread.Sleep(2000)

            driver.Quit()

            driver.Quit()

            Console.ReadLine()

    End Try

End Sub
```

2.2. Explaination

Above program starts with Imports statement. Imports statement is used to bring the classes from particular namespace in the scope of current program.

Imports OpenQA.Selenium

For example above statement will bring all classes defined in the OpenQA.Selenium namespace in the context of the current program.

All VB.Net applications have to be included in the module. So we have created the module called Module1.

Next statement defines Main sub routine which is the starting point for the program.

we have declared new variable driver of the interface type – IwebDriver. Next line starts with try statement. For now, you can ignore this line as I am going to explain this in more detail in exception handling chapter.

driver = new ChromeDriver(@"F:\selenium\csharp")

Above statement will make the driver variable refer to the new browser instance. Please note that ChromeDriver constructor takes the path of the chrome driver exe.

driver.Url = "http://www.google.co.in"

Above statement will set the url property of the driver to the site we want to open and test.

```
driver.Manage().Window.Maximize()
driver.Navigate()
```

Above 2 statements will maximize the browser window and then open www.google.co.in website in it.

In short we have created the instance of the Chrome webdriver and navigated to the given url.

Below code snippets show how to create the webdriver instance for the Firefox and IE.

```
Dim x As IwebDriver

x = new
InternetExplorerDriver(@"F:\selenium\csharp")

  x = New FirefoxDriver()
```

3. Identifying the elements in SELENIUM

As illustrated in the first program, It is very simple to create the webdriver instance and navigate to the webpage. In testing web application we need to perform operations on the webpage like clicking on the link or button, selecting the checkbox or radiobutton, choosing an item from the dropdown etc.

In selenium terminology, all objects in webpage are treated as webelements. So it is very important to identify the elements first and then perform some operations on them. Selenium provides plenty of methods to identify the web elements as mentioned below.

- Xpath
- CSS
- LinkText
- Name
- Id
- Class Name
- tagName
- partial link text

We are going to look into each of these methods one by one.

3.1.Xpath

Xpath is the web technology/standard that is used to access elements from the webpage or xml document. Detailed discussion of the xpath is beyond the scope of this book. We will see just simple examples to give you the idea of xpath. You can learn the basics of xpath at http://www.w3schools.com/xpath/xpath_syntax.asp

Examples – Suppose you want to identify the link of which href attribute contains google.

Xpath expression for above example -
//a[contains(@href,'google')]

Below code will find the first link of which **href** attribute contains google

```
driver.FindElement(By.XPath("//a[contains(@href,'
google')]")).Click()
```

Below table shows some commonly used xpath expressions.

Find all elements with tag input	//input
Find all input tag element having attribute type = 'hidden'	//input[@type='hidden']
Find all input tag element having attribute type = 'hidden' and name attribute = 'ren'	//input[@type='hidden'][@name='ren']
Find all input tag element with attribute type containing 'hid'	//input[contains(@type,'hid')]
Find all input tag element with attribute type starting with 'hid'	//input[starts-with(@type,'hid')]

Find all elements having innertext = 'password'	`//*[text()='Password']`
Find all td elements having innertext = 'password'	`//td[text()='Password']`
Find all next siblings of td tag having innertext = 'gender'	`//td[text()='Gender']//following-sibling::*`
Find all elements in the 2nd next sibling of td tag having innertext = 'gender'	`//td[text()='Gender']//following-sibling::*[2]//*`
Find input elements in the 2nd next sibling of td tag having innertext = 'gender'	`//td[text()='Gender']//following-sibling::*[2]//input`
Find the td which contains font element containing the text '12'	`//td[font[contains(text(),'12')]]`
Find all the preceding siblings of the td which contains font element containing the text '12'	`//td[font[contains(text(),'12')]]//preceding-sibling::*`

You can also use below tools to learn xpath
1. XPath Checker
2. Firebug.

In google chrome, you can copy the xpath of any element very easily. Below fig shows how we can do it.

Figure 7 - Copy xpath and CSS path in Chrome

In other browsers like IE and FF also, you will find similar options in developer tools.

You can also use console window to try and test xpath and CSS expressions from the console window provided in chrome.

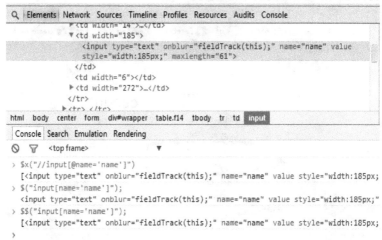

Figure 8 - Console window in chrome

To test xpath expressions, you can use below syntax.
```
$x("//input[@name='name']")
```

To test CSS expressions, you can use below syntax. $ will return only first matched element.
```
$("input[name='name']")
```

To test CSS expressions, you can use below syntax. $$ will return all matched elements.
```
$$("input[name='name']")
```

3.2.CSS

CSS selectors can also be used to find the web elements in a web page. You can visit
http://www.w3schools.com/cssref/css_selectors.asp to learn about css selectors.

```
Dim we As IwebElement
```

```
    we =
driver.FindElement(By.CssSelector("#shadow"))

    we.Click()
```

Above code will identify the first element having id equal to "**shadow**" and then click on it.

Below table shows some commonly used css Selector expressions.

Find all elements with tag input	input
Find all input tag element having attribute type = 'hidden'	input[type='hidden']
Find all input tag element having attribute type = 'hidden' and name attribute = 'ren'	input[type='hidden'][name='ren']
Find all input tag element with attribute type containing 'hid'	input[type*='hid']
Find all input tag element with attribute type starting with 'hid'	input[type^='hid']
Find all input tag element with attribute type ending with 'den'	input[type$='den']

3.3.LinkText

This method can be used to identify only links in the web page.

Example – Suppose you want to click on the link "news". You can use below syntax to click on the link.

```
    Dim we As IwebElement

    we = driver.FindElement(By.LinkText
("news"))

    We.Click()
```

3.4.Name

This method can be used to identify any object in the web page.

Only requirement is that the object should have a name attribute associated with it.

Example – Suppose you want to click on the button with name "submit". You can use below syntax to click on the button.

```
    Dim we As IwebElement

    we =
driver.FindElement(By.Name("submit"))

    we.Click()
```

3.5.Id

This method can be used to identify any object in the web page.

Only requirement is that the object should have a id attribute associated with it.

Example – Suppose you want to click on the button having id as "next". You can use below syntax to click on the button.

```
Dim we As IWebElement
    we = driver.FindElement(By.Id("next"))
```

3.6.Class Name

This method can be used to identify any object in the web page.

Only requirement is that the object should have a class attribute associated with it.

Example – Suppose you want to click on the button having class as "highlight". You can use below syntax to click on the button.

```
Dim we As IWebElement
    we =
driver.FindElement(By.ClassName("highlight"))
```

3.7.Tag Name

This method can be used to identify any element in the web page with given tag.

Example – Suppose you want to click on the first link. You can use below code.

```
Dim we As IwebElement

    we = driver.FindElement(By.TagName("A"))
```

3.8.Partial Link Text

This method can be used to identify only links in the web page.

Example – Suppose you want to click on the link with the text "google news". You can use below code.

```
Dim we As IwebElement

we =
driver.FindElement(By.PartialLinkText("news"))
```

4. Performing User Actions in Selenium

Performing user actions involves identification of the elements on the webpage and then doing some operation like clicking on the button, entering the data in the editboxes, selecting a value from the drop down.

4.1. Entering data in Editboxes

We can enter the data in the editboxes using sendkeys method as illustrated in the below example.

```
Imports System
Imports System.Collections.Generic
Imports System.Linq
Imports System.Text
Imports System.Threading
Imports OpenQA.Selenium
Imports OpenQA.Selenium.Firefox
Imports OpenQA.Selenium.Chrome
Imports OpenQA.Selenium.IE
Imports System.Collections.ObjectModel

Module Selenium

    Sub launchchrome()
        Dim driver As IWebDriver
        driver = Nothing

        Try

            driver = New
ChromeDriver("F:\selenium\csharp")

            driver.Url =
"http://register.rediff.com/register/register.p
hp"
```

```vb
driver.Manage().Timeouts().ImplicitlyWait(TimeS
pan.FromSeconds(20))

        driver.Navigate()

        'enter data in first name

driver.FindElement(By.Name("name")).SendKeys("s
alunke")

        Catch e As Exception

            Console.WriteLine("Exception
....*{0}", e.ToString())


        Finally
            Thread.Sleep(2000)

            driver.Quit()

            Console.ReadLine()

        End Try
    End Sub
End Module
```

4.2. Selecting a value from the Combo boxes.

We can select the value from the dropdown using 3 methods

1. SelectByText method
2. SelectByIndex method
3. SelectByValue method

You can use any of these methods to select a value from the dropdown.

```vbnet
Imports System
Imports System.Collections.Generic
Imports System.Linq
Imports System.Text
Imports System.Threading
Imports OpenQA.Selenium
Imports OpenQA.Selenium.Firefox
Imports OpenQA.Selenium.Chrome
Imports OpenQA.Selenium.IE
Imports OpenQA.Selenium.Support.UI
Imports System.Collections.ObjectModel

Module Module1

    Sub Main()
        Dim driver As IWebDriver
        driver = Nothing

        Try

        driver = New
ChromeDriver("F:\selenium\csharp")
        driver.Url = "http://www.amazon.in"

driver.Manage().Timeouts().ImplicitlyWait(TimeS
pan.FromSeconds(20))

            driver.Navigate()

            ' enter data in google search box

            Dim e As IwebDriver
```

```
            e =
driver.FindElement(By.XPath("//*[@id='searchDro
pdownBox']"))

            Dim select1 As SelectElement

            select1 = New SelectElement(e)
            'select the value Books from the
combo box
            select1.SelectByText("Books")

        Catch e As Exception

Console.WriteLine("Exception …****{0}",
e.ToString())

        Finally

            Thread.Sleep(2000)

            driver.Quit()

            Console.ReadLine()

        End Try
    End Sub
End Module
```

4.3. Clicking on Web Buttons in

We can click on the buttons using click method as illustrated in the below example.

```
Imports System
```

```vb
Imports System.Collections.Generic
Imports System.Linq
Imports System.Text
Imports System.Threading
Imports OpenQA.Selenium
Imports OpenQA.Selenium.Firefox
Imports OpenQA.Selenium.Chrome
Imports OpenQA.Selenium.IE
Imports OpenQA.Selenium.Support.UI
Imports System.Collections.ObjectModel

Module Module1

    Sub Main()
        Dim driver As IWebDriver
        driver = Nothing

        Try

        driver = New
ChromeDriver("F:\selenium\csharp")

        driver.Url = "http://www.amazon.in"

driver.Manage().Timeouts().ImplicitlyWait(TimeS
pan.FromSeconds(20))

            driver.Navigate()

            'enter data in google search box
            Dim e As IwebElement

            e =
driver.FindElement(By.XPath("//*[@id='twotabsea
rchtextbox']"))

            e.SendKeys("Selenium")

            Dim e1 As IwebElement
```

```
e1 = driver.FindElement(By.XPath("//*[@id='nav-
bar-inner']/div/form/div[2]/input"))

            'click on the button
            e1.click()


        Catch e As Exception

    Console.WriteLine("Exception .**{0}",
e.ToString())


        Finally

            Thread.Sleep(2000)

            driver.Quit()

            Console.ReadLine()

        End Try
    End Sub
End Module
```

4.4.Clicking on links

We can click on the links using click method just like how
we click on the buttons as illustrated in the below
example.

```
Imports System
Imports System.Collections.Generic
Imports System.Linq
Imports System.Text
Imports System.Threading
Imports OpenQA.Selenium
Imports OpenQA.Selenium.Firefox
Imports OpenQA.Selenium.Chrome
Imports OpenQA.Selenium.IE
```

```vbnet
Imports OpenQA.Selenium.Support.UI
Imports System.Collections.ObjectModel

Module Module1

    Sub Main()
        Dim driver As IWebDriver
        driver = Nothing

        Try

            driver = New
ChromeDriver("F:\selenium\csharp")

            driver.Url = "http://www.amazon.in"

driver.Manage().Timeouts().ImplicitlyWait(TimeS
pan.FromSeconds(20))

            driver.Navigate()

            'enter data in google search box
            Dim e1 As IWebElement

            e1 =
driver.FindElement(By.LinkText("Sell"))

            'click on the link sell

            e1.click()

        Catch e As Exception

    Console.WriteLine("Exception ..**{0}",
e.ToString())

        Finally

            Thread.Sleep(2000)
```

```
            driver.Quit()

            Console.ReadLine()

        End Try

    End Sub

End Module
```

4.5.Setting on/off checkboxes

We can first see if the checkbox is selected using isselected method. Then using click method we can perform the operations such as selecting or deselecting the checkboxes as illustrated in the below example.

```vb
Imports System
Imports System.Collections.Generic
Imports System.Linq
Imports System.Text
Imports System.Threading
Imports OpenQA.Selenium
Imports OpenQA.Selenium.Firefox
Imports OpenQA.Selenium.Chrome
Imports OpenQA.Selenium.IE
Imports OpenQA.Selenium.Support.UI
Imports System.Collections.ObjectModel

Module Module1

    Sub Main()
        Dim driver As IWebDriver
        driver = Nothing

        Try
```

```vb
        driver = New
ChromeDriver("F:\selenium\csharp")

    driver.Url = "https://www.gmail.com"

driver.Manage().Timeouts().ImplicitlyWait(TimeS
pan.FromSeconds(20))

        driver.Navigate()

        'enter data in google search box
        Dim e1 As IWebElement

        e1 =
driver.FindElement(By.XPath("//*[@id='Persisten
tCookie']"))

        'click on the link sell

        If e1.Selected Then
            'deselect checkbox
            e1.Click()
        Else
            'select checkbox
            e1.Click()

        End If

    Catch e As Exception

   Console.WriteLine("Exception ..**{0}",
e.ToString())

    Finally

        Thread.Sleep(2000)

        driver.Quit()

        Console.ReadLine()
```

```
        End Try

    End Sub

End Module
```

4.6. Selecting the radiobutton

We can select the radiobutton using click method as illustrated in the below example.

```vbnet
Imports System
Imports System.Collections.Generic
Imports System.Linq
Imports System.Text
Imports System.Threading
Imports OpenQA.Selenium
Imports OpenQA.Selenium.Firefox
Imports OpenQA.Selenium.Chrome
Imports OpenQA.Selenium.IE
Imports OpenQA.Selenium.Support.UI
Imports System.Collections.ObjectModel

Module Module1

    Sub Main()
        Dim driver As IWebDriver
        driver = Nothing

        Try

    driver = New
ChromeDriver("F:\selenium\csharp")

driver.Url =
http://register.rediff.com/register/register.ph
p
```

```vb.net
driver.Manage().Timeouts().ImplicitlyWait(TimeS
pan.FromSeconds(20))

        driver.Navigate()

    'select the radio button on rediff
register page
        Dim e1 As IWebElement

        e1 =
driver.FindElement(By.XPath("//*[@id='wrapper']
/table[2]/tbody/tr[21]/td[3]/input[2]"))

        e1.Click()

    Catch e As Exception

  Console.WriteLine("Exception ..**{0}",
e.ToString())

    Finally

        Thread.Sleep(2000)

        driver.Quit()

        Console.ReadLine()

    End Try

  End Sub

End Module
```

5. Reading data from webpage in Selenium

Selenium VB API provides 2 important methods to read data from web elements.

1. **GetCssValue** – gets the value of css property of the element
2. **GetAttribute** – gets the value of given attribute.

We can also find the innertext of the element using Text property.

We can also check if

1. Element is displayed using Displayed property
2. Element is selected using Selected property
3. Element is enabled using Enabled property

Examples –

Below statement will print the width of the element having name login.

```
Dim x As String
x =
driver.FindElement(By.Name("login")).GetCssValu
e("width")
```

Below statement will print the value of the attribute onfocus of the element having name login.

```
Dim x As String
 x =
driver.FindElement(By.Name("login")).GetAttribu
te("onfocus")
```

Below statement will print true if the checkbox with name choice is selected.

```
Dim x As Boolean
   x =
driver.FindElement(By.Name("choice")).Selected(
)
```

Below statement will print true if the radiobutton with name Gender is displayed on the current webpage.

```
Dim x As Boolean
   x =
driver.FindElement(By.Name("Gender")).Displayed
()
```

Below statement will print true if the button with name add is enabled.

```
Dim x As Boolean
   x =
driver.FindElement(By.Name("add")).Enabled()
```

5.1.Reading data from Editboxes

We can get the data from editbox using GetAttribute Method as illustrated in the below example.

```
Imports System
Imports System.Collections.Generic
Imports System.Linq
Imports System.Text
Imports System.Threading
Imports OpenQA.Selenium
Imports OpenQA.Selenium.Firefox
Imports OpenQA.Selenium.Chrome
Imports OpenQA.Selenium.IE
Imports OpenQA.Selenium.Support.UI
```

```vb.net
Imports System.Collections.ObjectModel

Module Module1

    Sub Main()

        Dim driver As IwebDriver

        driver = Nothing

        Try

        driver = New
ChromeDriver("F:\selenium\csharp")

            driver.Url =
"http://register.rediff.com/register/register.p
hp"


driver.Manage().Timeouts().ImplicitlyWait(TimeS
pan.FromSeconds(20))

driver.Manage().Timeouts().SetPageLoadTimeout(T
imeSpan.FromSeconds(50))

            driver.Manage().Window.Maximize()

            driver.Navigate()

            Dim e As IWebElement
            'e = null

            Thread.Sleep(1000)

            e =
driver.FindElement(By.Name("name"))

            e.SendKeys("sagar")
```

```
Console.WriteLine("Text displayed is ->{0} ",
e.GetAttribute("value"))

        Catch e As Exception

            Console.WriteLine("Exception
..**{0}", e.ToString())

        Finally

            Thread.Sleep(2000)

            driver.Quit()

            Console.ReadLine()

        End Try

    End Sub

End Module
```

5.2.Reading data from combo boxes

We can get the data from combobox using Text property
as illustrated in the below example.

```
Imports System
Imports System.Collections.Generic
Imports System.Linq
Imports System.Text
Imports System.Threading
Imports OpenQA.Selenium
Imports OpenQA.Selenium.Firefox
Imports OpenQA.Selenium.Chrome
```

```vbnet
Imports OpenQA.Selenium.IE
Imports OpenQA.Selenium.Support.UI
Imports System.Collections.ObjectModel

Module Module1

    Sub Main()

        Dim driver As IwebDriver

        driver = Nothing

        Try

        driver = New
ChromeDriver("F:\selenium\csharp")

            driver.Url =
"http://register.rediff.com/register/register.p
hp"

driver.Manage().Timeouts().ImplicitlyWait(TimeS
pan.FromSeconds(20))

driver.Manage().Timeouts().SetPageLoadTimeout(T
imeSpan.FromSeconds(50))

            driver.Manage().Window.Maximize()

            driver.Navigate()

            Dim e As IWebElement

            'e = null

            Thread.Sleep(5000)

            'get the value selected in month
drop down rediff page.
```

```
            e =
driver.FindElement(By.Name("DOB_Month"))

            Dim se As SelectElement

            se = New SelectElement(e)


Console.WriteLine(se.SelectedOption.Text)

        Catch e As Exception

            Console.WriteLine("Exception
..**{0}", e.ToString())

        Finally

            Thread.Sleep(2000)

            driver.Quit()

            Console.ReadLine()

        End Try

    End Sub

End Module
```

5.3.Reading data from checkboxes

We can see if the checkbox is selected or not using
Selected as illustrated in the below example.

```
Imports System
Imports System.Collections.Generic
Imports System.Linq
```

```vb.net
Imports System.Text
Imports System.Threading
Imports OpenQA.Selenium
Imports OpenQA.Selenium.Firefox
Imports OpenQA.Selenium.Chrome
Imports OpenQA.Selenium.IE
Imports OpenQA.Selenium.Support.UI
Imports System.Collections.ObjectModel

Module Module1

    Sub Main()

        Dim driver As IwebDriver

        driver = Nothing

        Try

        driver = New
ChromeDriver("F:\selenium\csharp")

            driver.Url =
"http://register.rediff.com/register/register.p
hp"


driver.Manage().Timeouts().ImplicitlyWait(TimeS
pan.FromSeconds(20))

driver.Manage().Timeouts().SetPageLoadTimeout(T
imeSpan.FromSeconds(50))

            driver.Manage().Window.Maximize()

            driver.Navigate()

            Dim e As IWebElement

            'IWebElement e=null
```

```
            Thread.Sleep(5000)

                'verify if checkbox is selected or
not.

            e =
driver.FindElement(By.Name("chk_altemail"))
            Console.WriteLine("Checkbox is selected
?{0}", e.Selected)

        Catch e As Exception

            Console.WriteLine("Exception
..**{0}", e.ToString())

        Finally

            Thread.Sleep(2000)

            driver.Quit()

            Console.ReadLine()

        End Try

    End Sub

End Module
```

5.4.Reading data from Radio Buttons

We can see if the radiobutton is selected or not using
Selected property as illustrated in the below example.

```
Imports System
Imports System.Collections.Generic
Imports System.Linq
```

```vbnet
Imports System.Text
Imports System.Threading
Imports OpenQA.Selenium
Imports OpenQA.Selenium.Firefox
Imports OpenQA.Selenium.Chrome
Imports OpenQA.Selenium.IE
Imports OpenQA.Selenium.Support.UI
Imports System.Collections.ObjectModel


Module Module1

    Sub Main()

        Dim driver As IwebDriver

        driver = Nothing

        Try

        driver = New
ChromeDriver("F:\selenium\csharp")

            driver.Url =
"http://register.rediff.com/register/register.p
hp"


driver.Manage().Timeouts().ImplicitlyWait(TimeS
pan.FromSeconds(20))

driver.Manage().Timeouts().SetPageLoadTimeout(T
imeSpan.FromSeconds(50))

            driver.Manage().Window.Maximize()

            driver.Navigate()

            Dim e As IWebElement

            'IWebElement e=null;
```

```vb.net
            Thread.Sleep(5000)

        Dim ec As ReadOnlyCollection(Of
IWebElement)

        ec =
driver.FindElements(By.Name("gender"))

        Dim k As Integer

        For k = 0 To UBound(ec.ToArray)
        Console.WriteLine("which gender
selected ?{0}", ec(k).Selected)

        Next

    Catch e As Exception

        Console.WriteLine("Exception
..**{0}", e.ToString())

    Finally

        Thread.Sleep(2000)

        driver.Quit()

        Console.ReadLine()

    End Try

  End Sub

End Module
```

5.5.Working with Tables in SELENIUM

Reading the data from the table is very easy in selenium webdriver.

We can identify the table using name, Id or xpath and then we can access the rows one by one using findElements method.

For example – below statement will find all row elements from the given table. Please note that t stands for the table object you have found using findElement method.

```vbnet
        Dim driver As IWebDriver
        Dim ec As ReadOnlyCollection(Of
IWebElement)
        ec =
driver.FindElements(By.TagName("tr"))
```

6. Synchronization in SELENIUM

We can use below synchronization methods in selenium.

6.1. Page Load Synchrnoization

We can set the default page navigation timeout. Below statement will set the navigation timeout as 50. This means that selenium script will wait for maximum 50 seconds for page to load. If page does not load within 50 seconds, it will throw an exception.

```
driver.Manage().Timeouts().SetPageLoadTimeout(T
imeSpan.FromSeconds(50))
```

6.2. Element Synchronization

We can set the default element existance timeout. Below statement will set the default object synchronization timeout as 20. This means that selenium script will wait for maximum 20 seconds for element to exist. If Web element does not exist within 20 seconds, it will throw an exception.

```
driver.manage().timeouts().implicitlyWait(20,
TimeUnit.SECONDS)
```

6.3. Synchronization based upon specific condition

We can also instruct selenium to wait until element is in one of the expected conditions mentioned below.

1. ElementExists
2. ElementIsVisible
3. TitleContains

4. Titleis

For example, below code will wait until the element with id – "dd" exists in the application. Timeout for this condition check is 20 seconds and while waiting driver will ignore the exceptions as coded in the second statement.

```
Dim w As WebDriverWait

w = New WebDriverWait(driver,
TimeSpan.FromSeconds(20))

w.IgnoreExceptionTypes(typeof(StaleElementRefer
enceException),typeof(InvalidElementStateExcept
ion))

w.IgnoreExceptionTypes(TypeOf(StaleElementRefer
enceException),TypeOf(InvalidElementStateExcept
ion ))

w.Until(ExpectedConditions.ElementExists(By.Id(
"dd")))
```

7. Advanced Operations in Selenium

7.1. Mouse Events in SELENIUM

We can simulate many events in selenium using Actions class defined in using OpenQA.Selenium.Interactions namespace.

1. Click
2. ClickAndHold
3. ContextClick
4. DoubleClick
5. DragAndDrop
6. KeyUp
7. KeyDown

Below code will Double click on the given element - e.

```vbnet
Dim e As IWebElement

e=driver.FindElement(By.Name("showdetail"))

        Dim a As Actions

        a = New Actions(driver)

        a.DoubleClick(e).Perform()
```

We can perform other actions in similar fashion.

7.2.Taking Screen shots in SELENIUM

Below code will illustrate how we can take screen shots in selenium in VB.Net.

Please note that we will have to add a reference of the System.Drawing and then import Imaging Class
```
Imports System.Drawing.Imaging
```

Complete Example is given below

```vbnet
Imports System.Text
Imports System.Threading
Imports OpenQA.Selenium
Imports OpenQA.Selenium.Firefox
Imports OpenQA.Selenium.Chrome
Imports OpenQA.Selenium.IE
Imports OpenQA.Selenium.Support.UI
Imports System.Collections.ObjectModel
Imports System.Drawing.Imaging

Module Module1

    Sub Main()

        Dim driver As IwebDriver

        driver = Nothing

        Try

        driver = New
ChromeDriver("F:\selenium\csharp")

            driver.Url =
"http://register.rediff.com/register/register.p
hp"
```

```
driver.Manage().Timeouts().ImplicitlyWait(TimeS
pan.FromSeconds(20))

driver.Manage().Timeouts().SetPageLoadTimeout(T
imeSpan.FromSeconds(50))

        driver.Manage().Window.Maximize()

        driver.Navigate()


  Dim x As ITakesScreenshot

        x = driver


x.GetScreenshot().SaveAsFile("d:\photos\vb.png"
, ImageFormat.Png)

        Catch e As Exception

            Console.WriteLine("Exception
..**{0}", e.ToString())

        Finally

            Thread.Sleep(2000)

            driver.Quit()

            Console.ReadLine()

        End Try

    End Sub

End Module
```

7.3.Executing Java Script in SELENIUM

Below code will illustrate how we can execute Java script with webdriver in VB.Net.

We can use IjavaScriptExecutor interface to execute java script

```vbnet
Imports System.Text
Imports System.Threading
Imports OpenQA.Selenium
Imports OpenQA.Selenium.Firefox
Imports OpenQA.Selenium.Chrome
Imports OpenQA.Selenium.IE
Imports OpenQA.Selenium.Support.UI
Imports System.Collections.ObjectModel

Module Module1

    Sub Main()

        Dim driver As IwebDriver

        driver = Nothing

        Try

        driver = New
ChromeDriver("F:\selenium\csharp")

            driver.Url =
"http://register.rediff.com/register/register.p
hp"


driver.Manage().Timeouts().ImplicitlyWait(TimeS
pan.FromSeconds(20))
```

```vbnet
driver.Manage().Timeouts().SetPageLoadTimeout(T
imeSpan.FromSeconds(50))

        driver.Manage().Window.Maximize()

        driver.Navigate()


  Dim x As IJavaScriptExecutor
        x = driver

        Dim src As String =
x.ExecuteScript("return
document.documentElement.innerHTML")

        Console.WriteLine(src)


        Catch e As Exception

            Console.WriteLine("Exception
..**{0}", e.ToString())

        Finally

            Thread.Sleep(2000)

            driver.Quit()

            Console.ReadLine()

        End Try

    End Sub

End Module
```

8. Frames, Alerts and Windows in SELENIUM

8.1. Handling Frames

To work with frames we need to switch to the frame and then perform the operation inside it. We can switch to the frame using 3 ways in VB selenium API.

1. Using frame Index
2. Using frame name
3. Identifying a frame by any other method like id, class etc.

For example –

```
Dim driver As IwebDriver

Dim e As IwebElement

driver.SwitchTo().Frame(1)
 'Above code will switch to the first frame in
web page

            e =
driver.FindElement(By.Id("bpl"))

            driver.SwitchTo().Frame(e)
 'Above code will switch to the frame with id
bpl

            driver.SwitchTo().Frame("f1")
 'Above code will switch to the frame having
name - f1.
```

Once you switch to the desired frame, you can do rest of the operations the same way as you do in single document page.

8.2.Working with Alerts and Windows

We can handle alerts using **Alert class in VB.Net** Web Driver.

At first, we need to get the alert reference using below syntax.

```
Dim alert As IAlert

 alert = driver.SwitchTo().Alert()
 alert = driver.SwitchTo().Alert()
```

Then we can click on Ok button using below syntax.

```
alert.Accept()
```

Then we can click on Cancel button using below syntax.

```
alert.Dismiss()
```

To get the text displayed in the alert, you can use Text Property

```
Dim text As String
text = alert.Text()
```

We can get the enter data in the editbox displayed inside the alert using below code

```
driver.SwitchTo().Alert().SendKeys("abc")
```

Below code will show you how we can handle pop up windows in selenium in VB.Net.

Ok. Now let us see how to work with the **mulitple windows in Selenium VB.**

```
//***********************************************
//below statemewnt will click on link
// and it will open new window
```

```
driver.FindElement(By.Id("link")).Click()

        Dim popWindowHandle As String
        popWindowHandle = ""

        'get the current window handles
        Dim mainWindow As String

        mainWindow =
driver.CurrentWindowHandle

        'get the collection of all open
windows
    Dim windowHandles As ReadOnlyCollection(Of
String)
        windowHandles =
driver.WindowHandles

        For Each handle As String In
windowHandles
        If (handle <> mainWindow) Then
            popWindowHandle = handle

            Exit For

        End If
```

```
        Next


        'switch to new pop up window
        'and perform any operation you want to
perform

driver.SwitchTo().Window(popWindowHandle)

    'Print the title of new pop up window just
opened.
                Console.WriteLine(driver.Title)
                driver.Close()

            'switch back to original window

driver.SwitchTo().Window(mainWindow)
```

9. Important Built-in Function in VB.Net.

9.1. Working with Strings in VB.Net

We must know below string operations while working with selenium.

```vbnet
Imports System
Imports System.Collections.Generic
Imports System.Linq
Imports System.Text
Imports OpenQA.Selenium
Imports OpenQA.Selenium.IE
Imports OpenQA.Selenium.Support.UI
Imports System.Collections.ObjectModel
Imports OpenQA.Selenium.Interactions
Imports System.Globalization

Module MyString

    Sub stringfunctions()

        Try
            'To find the length of the string
            Console.WriteLine("Length of sagar ->{0}
", "sagar".Length)

            'To find the n characters from the left
side
            Console.WriteLine("Left 3 char of sagar
-> {0} ", "sagar".Substring(0, 3))

            'To find the last n characters of the
string
            Console.WriteLine("Last 2 char of sagar
->{0} ", "sagar".Substring("sagar".Length - 2, 2))

            'To convert the string to upper case
            Console.WriteLine("String - sagar
salunke in upper case is -> {0} ", "sagar
salunke".ToUpper())
```

```vb
                'To convert the string to lower case
            Console.WriteLine("String - SAGAR
SALUNKE in lower case is ->{0} ", "SAGAR
SALUNKE".ToLower())

                'To check if the string starts with
specified sub string
            Console.WriteLine("String - sagar
salunke starts with sagar? ->{0} ", "sagar
salunke".StartsWith("sagar"))

                'How to replace the string with other
string
            Console.WriteLine("sagar salunke
replaced by ganesh salunke -> {0} ", "sagar
salunke".Replace("sagar", "ganesh"))

                'Check if the given substring exists in
string
            Console.WriteLine("sagar salunke
contains sagar?{0} ", "sagar
salunke".Contains("sagar"))

                'check for the equality of the string
            Console.WriteLine("Result of comparison
of sa with Sa -> {0} ", "sa".Equals("Sa",
StringComparison.OrdinalIgnoreCase))

                'join 2 string in array
            Dim p() As String = {"sachin",
"tendulkar"}
            Console.WriteLine("String after joining
-> {0} ", String.Join(" ", p))

                'convert the string to array
            Dim ar() As Char
            ar = "sagar".ToArray()
            Console.WriteLine("String converted to
array - sagar -> {0}", ar(2))

                'split the string by any character say *
            Dim s() As String
            s = "sa*gar".Split("*")
```

```vbnet
            Console.WriteLine("sa*gar splitted with
* ->{0}", s(0))

            'Remove the string
            Console.WriteLine("sagar salunke
replace".Remove(0, 3))

            'Insert the string
            Console.WriteLine("Inserted string is -
>{0}", "Ram Sham".Insert(4, "and "))

            'return the mid String
            Dim m As String = Mid("Selenium
webdriver in vb.net", 10, 9)
            Console.WriteLine(m)

            'Trim
            'Remove the left and right space
            Console.WriteLine("Trim is -> {0}", "
Selenium    ".Trim())
            'remove only right space
            Console.WriteLine("{0}", "  Selenium
".TrimEnd())
            'Remove only left space
            Console.WriteLine("{0}", "  Selenium
".TrimStart())

            'Print string in new line
            Console.WriteLine("{0}", "[First" +
Environment.NewLine + "Second]")
            ' Console.WriteLine("{0}", )

            'adding spaces to the right and left
            Console.WriteLine("[{0}]", LSet("test",
10))
            Console.WriteLine("[{0}]", RSet("test",
10))

            'Index of
            Console.WriteLine("Index of is ->{0}",
"Selenium web driver".IndexOf("w"))
            'Last Index of
            Console.WriteLine("Last index is{0}",
"Selenium web driver".LastIndexOf("d"))
```

```
                'first letter of each word uppercase
                'Imports System.Globalization
                Console.WriteLine("First latter Capital
->{0}",
CultureInfo.CurrentCulture.TextInfo.ToTitleCase("sel
enium web driver"))

        Catch ee As Exception
                Console.WriteLine("Exception ..**{0}",
ee.ToString())

        Finally

                Console.ReadLine()

        End Try

    End Sub

End Module
```

9.2. Working with Date and Time

In all banking projects, you will have to calculate the date differences or find the future or past date. So you must know how to do this in VB.Net.

```
Module Mydatetime

    Sub Main()

        'print current system time and date
        Console.WriteLine(DateTime.Now)

        'convert the string to date
        Dim d As DateTime

        d = New DateTime()
```

```
        d = DateTime.Parse("09-jan-1986")

    'convert the string to date using parseexact
method
    d = DateTime.ParseExact("09/01/1986",
"dd/MM/yyyy",
System.Globalization.CultureInfo.InvariantCultu
re)

        'Get future date and Change the date
format in VB

Console.WriteLine(d.Add(TimeSpan.FromDays(1)).T
oString("dd/MM/yyyy"))

        'Get past date and Change the date
format in VB
        Console.WriteLine(d.Add(TimeSpan.FromDays
(-1)).ToString("dd/MM/yyyy"))


    End Sub
End Module
```

9.3. Working with Files and Folders

Creating text files in VB is very simple with the help of File
Class. Below lines of code illustrate how we can read as
well as append the text data to a file.

```
Imports System

Imports System.IO

Module Myfilesandfolder

    Sub filefolder()
```

```
        'Create text file
        Dim fi As StreamWriter
        Dim f As StreamWriter

        fi = File.CreateText("d:\abc.txt")

        fi.WriteLine("Sagar shivaji salunke")
        fi.Close()

        'read text file

Console.WriteLine(File.ReadAllText("d:\abc.txt"
))

        'append data

        f = File.AppendText("d:\abc.txt")

        f.WriteLine("Hello Baby")

        f.Close()

    End Sub

End Module
```

9.4. Maths

Important Maths related methods provided in VB.Net are given below.

1. Round - rounds the number to specific number of decimals.
2. Pow - to find value of x^y.

```
Module Mymath
```

```vb
Sub Main()

    Console.WriteLine(Math.Round(34.456, 2))
     'output will be 34.46

    Console.WriteLine(Math.Pow(2, 3))
     'output will be 8.

    Console.WriteLine(Math.Abs(-12.6))
     'output will be 12.6

    Console.WriteLine(Math.Cos(5))
     'output will be 0.283662185463226

    Console.WriteLine(Math.Equals(12, 6))
     'output will be False

    Console.WriteLine(Math.Max(10, 45))
     'output will be 45

    Console.WriteLine(Math.Min(2, 5))
     'output will be 2

    Console.WriteLine(Math.Sqrt(5))
     'output will be 2.23

    End Sub

End Module
```

10. Exception Handling in SELENIUM

Exception handling involves handling unexpected conditions in the programm.

For example – dividing any number by 0 throws the exception

```vbnet
Module Myexception

    Sub Main()

        Try
                Dim b As Integer
                Dim a As Integer

                b = 0
                a = 2 / b

        Catch e As Exception

                Console.WriteLine("Exception Type ->{0}", e.GetType().ToString())

                Console.WriteLine("Exception Source ->{0}", e.Source)

                Console.WriteLine("Exception Stacktrace ->{0}", e.StackTrace)

        End Try

    End Sub

End Module
```

Executing above program will produce below output. As displayed in the output the DivideByZeroException is generated and stacktrace also show the line number in the source file where the exception occurred.

```
Exception Type ->System.DivideByZeroException
Exception Source ->Selenium-IE
Exception Stacktrace ->    at Selenium_IE.topics.doop() in F:\selenium\SeleniumDr
iver\Selenium-IE\topics.cs:line 148
```

Please remember that we can have many catch blocks after try block. Whenever exception occurs, it is thrown and caught by the catch block. In catch block we can write the code for recovery.

11. Excel Programming in SELENIUM

VB provides a good support to do programming with
Microsoft excel workbooks. You will have to add a
reference of the excel library as shown in below figure.

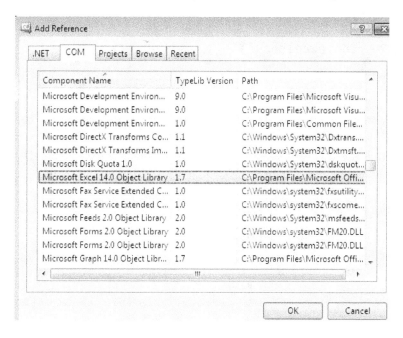

Figure 9 -Add reference of Excel Library

11.1. Creating and writing data to Excel Workbook

When we design a test automation framework in
Selenium, we usually store the test data inside excel
sheets.

Below example demonstrates how we can create and
write to excel workbook.

We need to create an excel application reference as shown in below program. Then we can access native properties and methods of Excel Automation object.

```vbnet
Imports Microsoft.Office.Interop.Excel

Module Excelworkbook

    Sub excelbook()

        Try

            Dim e As New
Microsoft.Office.Interop.Excel.Application()

            e.Visible = True

            e.DisplayAlerts = False

            Dim wb As Workbook =
e.Workbooks.Add()

            'get the reference of first sheet
in workbook added

            Dim ws As Worksheet =
wb.Worksheets(1)

            'write some data to cell 1,1
            ws.Cells(1, 1) = "salunke"

            'save the workbook to d drive.

            wb.SaveAs("d:\csbook.xlsx")

            wb.Close()

            e.Quit()
```

```vb
                'handle excpetions in any.
        Catch ex As Exception

            Console.WriteLine("Exception Type -
>{0}", ex.GetType().ToString())

            Console.WriteLine("Exception Source
->{0}", ex.Source)

            Console.WriteLine("Exception
Stacktrace ->{0}", ex.StackTrace)

        End Try

    End Sub
End Module
```

11.2. Reading data from existing workbook

We can read the data from excel sheets using below code.

```vb
Imports Microsoft.Office.Interop.Excel

Module Excelworkbook

    Sub excelbook()

        Dim e As New
Microsoft.Office.Interop.Excel.Application()

        Dim wb As Workbook

        Dim ws As Worksheet

        Try
            e = New
Microsoft.Office.Interop.Excel.Application()
```

```vbnet
                e.Visible = True

                e.DisplayAlerts = False

                wb =
e.Workbooks.Open("d:\csbook.xlsx")

                ws = wb.Worksheets(1)

                Console.WriteLine("Data in cell 1,1
-> {0}", (ws.Cells(1, 1).Value))

                wb.Close()
                e.Quit()

                'handle excpetions in any.
        Catch ex As Exception

                Console.WriteLine("Exception Type -
>{0}", ex.GetType().ToString())

                Console.WriteLine("Exception Source
->{0}", ex.Source)

                Console.WriteLine("Exception
Stacktrace ->{0}", ex.StackTrace)

        End Try

    End Sub

End Module
```

12. Framework Designing in SELENIUM

There are 3 types of automation frameworks that can be designed in selenium. Please note that In any other automation tools like QTP, Winrunner similar kinds of frameworks are popular.

Keyword Driven Framework :

In Keyword Driven Framework , Importance is given to functions than Test Data. when we have to test multiple functionality we can go for keyword frameworks. Each keyword is mapped to function in SELENIUM library and application.

DATA Driven Framework :

In data driven framework, importance is given to test data than multiple functionality of application. We design data driven framework to work with applications where we want to test same flow with different test data.

Hybrid Framework -

This is the combination of keyword and data driven frameworks.

After analyzing the application, you can decide what kind of framework best suits your needs and then you can design automation framework in SELENIUM.

Components of Keyword Driven framework

Keyword driven Automation Framework is most popular test automation framework. It is very easy to design and learn a keyword driven automation framework in SELENIUM.

In this article I will explain you all details about how we can design and use keyword driven automation framework in SELENIUM with example. I will also explain the advantages and disadvantages of keyword driven automation framework in SELENIUM.

In keyword driven automation framework, focus is mainly on kewords/functions and not the test data. This means we focus on creating the functions that are mapped to the functionality of the application.

For example - Suppose you have a flight reservation application which provides many features like

1. Login to the application

2. Search Flights

3. Book Flight tickets

4. Cancel Tickets

5. Fax Order

6. View Reports

To implement the keyword driven automation framework for this kind of application we will create functions in VB.Net for each functionality mentioned above. We pass the test data and test object details to these functions.

The main components of keyword driven automation framework in SELENIUM

Each keyword driven automation framework has some common components as mentioned below.

1. Scripts Library

2. Test Data (generally in excel format)

3. SELENIUM - Settings and Environment Variables

4. Reports - (Generally in HTML format)

5. Test Driver Script Method

Test Data Sheet in keyword driven framework in SELENIUM.

Generally automated test cases are stored in excel sheets. From SELENIUM script ,we read excel file and then row by row we execute the functions in a test case. Each test case is implemented as a set of keywords.

Common columns in Data sheet are mentioned below.

1. Test case ID - Stores the Test Case ID mapped to Manual Test Cases.

2. Test Case Name - Name of the Test cases/ Scenario.

3. Execute Flag - if Marked Y -> Test case will be executed

4. Test_Step_Id - Steps in a test case

5. Keyword - Mapped to function in library file.

6. Object Types - Class of the object e.g winedit, webedit, swfbutton etc

7. Object Names -Names of objects in OR .

8. Object Values - Actual test data to be entered in the objects.

9. Parameter1 - This is used to control the execution flow in the function.

Test_ID	TC_Name	Execute	Test_Step_ID	Keyword	Object_Types	Object_Names	Object_Values	Parameter1
1	Login To App	Y	Step1	login	winedit winedit	usend password	salunke mercury	
			Step2	Insert_Order	wincombobox wincombobo	flyfrom flyto	london paris	
			Step3	Fax_Order				Order_Id

Please note that this is just a sample data sheet that can be used in keyword driven framework. There could be customized data sheets for each project depending upon the requirement and design.

For example there could be more parameters or test data is stored in the databases.

Test Driver Script in SELENIUM.

This is the heart of keyword driven / data driven frameworks. This is the main script that interacts with all modules mentioned above.

Main tasks that are accomplished by driver script are ->

1. Read data from the Environment variables.

2. Call report module to create Report folders / files

3. Read Excel file

4. Call the function mapped to keyword.

5. Log the result